WHEN ESTHER MORRIS HEADED WEST

Women, Wyoming, and the Right to Vote

by CONNIE NORDHIELM WOOLDRIDGE

illustrated by JACQUELINE ROGERS

HOLIDAY HOUSE / New York

Special thanks to
Todd Guenther, Director of the Museum of the American West;
Scott Goetz and Tom Lindmier, South Pass City Historic Site;
Larry K. Brown and the staff at the Wyoming State Archives;
and Chris and Kevin Hagen.

Library of Congress Cataloging-in-Publication Data
Wooldridge, Connie Nordhielm.
When Esther Morris headed West: women, Wyoming, and the right to vote/
by Connie Nordhielm Wooldridge; illustrated by Jacqueline Rogers.
p. cm.
Includes bibliographical references.
ISBN 0-8234-1597-X
1. Morris, Esther Hobart, 1814–1902—Juvenile literature.
2. Suffragists—Wyoming—Biography—Juvenile literature.
3. Women justices of the peace—Wyoming—Biography—Juvenile literature.
4. Women—Suffrage—Wyoming—History—19th century—Juvenile literature.
[1. Morris, Esther Hobart, 1814–1902. 2. Justices of the peace.
3. Women—Biography. 4. Suffragists.]
I. Rogers, Jacqueline, ill. II. Title.
JK1899.M67 W99 2001
324.6'23'092—dc21
[B]   00-044875

Her name was Esther Mae Hobart McQuigg Slack Morris,
and in 1869 she headed out to South Pass City in the Wyoming Territory.
She was fifty-five years old.

South Pass City was a place that sprouted out of nearly nothing at the mention of the word "gold." The space around it was large and wide open. That was a good thing because Mrs. Morris was a large woman with wide-open ideas that needed more room than could be had in New York or Illinois, where she'd come from. You see, she thought a woman should be able to vote and hold office, the same as a man.

After she got herself settled in South Pass City, she paid a call on a man who had already argued hard for the same new and crazy-sounding idea she was bringing in from the East. That man was Colonel William Bright, and he thought women's being able to vote and hold office made all kinds of sense. Since he was an elected member of the Wyoming Territory Council, he proposed An Act to Grant to the Women of the Wyoming Territory the Right of Suffrage and to Hold Office.

Colonel Bright was opposed by a feisty young lawyer named Benjamin Sheeks, another representative from South Pass City, who thought the idea was hogwash. His plan was to keep the thing from ever being voted on at all. He made a motion to postpone discussion until July Fourth, which any fool knew was a holiday.

But Mr. Ben Sheeks lost the day, and the heretofore unheard-of up and happened. In the closing months of 1869, a legislature full of men voted to give the women of Wyoming rights no other women in the world had: They could vote and hold office the same as men.

"The deed is done," read one newspaper. "Ladies, prepare your ballots!" read another. "Reckless copperheads!" read a third, referring to the legislators who'd voted in such a fool thing. Back in South Pass City, the justice of the peace resigned.

Now that women had the right to vote, it was time to prove they could hold office just as well. Mrs. Morris had no hankering for power or highfalutin titles. But she knew an idea—even one voted into law—wasn't worth a hill of beans as long as it stayed words on a page. Her boys were grown and it was time to step away from her cooking and gardening for a spell and do a thing that might help women coming along later on. So Mrs. Morris applied for the position of South Pass City Justice of the Peace. The whole Wyoming Territory let out a gasp. But the only fellow who opposed her for the position failed to qualify. So there she was: a judge. And that made her the first female in the United States to hold a public office.

A test of her ability came early on from the very man she was replacing. He refused to hand over the court docket. He didn't think Mrs. Morris should have it. He didn't think any woman should have it.

"You can keep your dirty docket," Mrs. Morris told him, and got herself a nice clean one.

Then there was the time young Ben Sheeks, back to lawyering, argued a case in her court. The opposing attorney was having a heyday picking at every little thing and getting Mr. Sheeks's dander up real good. After he'd had about all he could take, Mr. Sheeks escorted his opponent out of the room when it didn't appear the fellow was of a mind to go.

When Mr. Sheeks came back into the courtroom, he knew he'd gone and done it. His views on the woman question were no secret and here he'd misbehaved in front of the first woman judge in the country. The situation called for humbleness and that was not a thing that came easy to Ben Sheeks.

"Your honor," he said, "I apologize for my behavior and I submit to any punishment you might inflict. I was in contempt."

Mrs. Morris was not educated in the fine points of the law. But she'd raised three sons in rough-and-tumble places, and she knew a thing or two about common-sense fairness. "Your behavior was justified, Mr. Sheeks," was all she said. And that was an end to it.

Along with seven other South Pass City women, the judge cast
her vote for the very first time on September 6, 1870.
She later claimed she had her personal physician by
her side, and he determined the operation of voting
had no ill effects on a woman's health.

Her term ended the following month. "My position as justice of the peace was a test to woman's ability to hold public office," she said, "and I feel that my work has been satisfactory, although I have often regretted I was not better qualified to fill the position. Like all pioneers, I have labored more in faith and hope." When she stepped down from the bench, Mrs. Morris handed the court docket over to the same judge who wouldn't turn his loose eight months before.

The gold fever that had brought three thousand people to South Pass City died down. Colonel Bright moved to Denver and then finished out his days in Washington, D.C.

Ben Sheeks headed for Salt Lake City and then west to
Washington State. Somewhere along the way he took up the crazy
notion that women should be able to vote and hold office the same
as men.

Mrs. Morris moved to Laramie,
Wyoming, and then on to Cheyenne.
She was close to ninety when she died.

In the summer of 1920, a professor from the University of Wyoming made her way out to what was left of South Pass City. She got herself a wheelbarrow and took a stone from the broken-down home of William Bright, who once had the courage to propose a crazy new idea.

She took another stone from the home of Esther Morris, who had the courage to show how the idea looked in the living of it. She took a third from the home of Ben Sheeks, who hated the idea, saw how it looked in the living, and had the courage to change his way of thinking.

The professor piled the stones into a monument and invited the remaining inhabitants of South Pass City to a dedication ceremony. As the sun sank behind the mountains, nineteen human beings, two dogs, and a cow remembered for a moment that once in time a thing bigger and better than gold had happened here.

In Washington, D.C., later that same summer of 1920, the Secretary of State announced a change to the United States Constitution. He said women in all states were now allowed to vote, the same as men.

It wasn't a new idea for the state of Wyoming.
The folks back East just took a little longer getting
to it is all.

AUTHOR'S NOTE

Women's suffrage became an organized movement at a convention held in Seneca Falls, New York, in 1848. But each time a state tried to pass a law giving women the right to vote, the attempt failed.

Supporters of women's suffrage began to look to the western territories where only a majority vote of the legislature and the governor's signature were required. Proposed laws were just barely voted down in Washington [1854], Nebraska [1856], and Dakota [1869] before the Wyoming Territorial Legislature succeeded in passing legislation giving women the vote [1869].

Twenty years later, the Wyoming Territory's suffrage law almost kept it from becoming a state. Wyoming's delegate to Washington, D.C., Joseph M. Carey, sent a frantic telegram home. He was afraid that if the suffrage law stayed a part of Wyoming's constitution, the United States Congress would turn down its bid for statehood.

The story goes that Carey received two telegrams in reply. The first was from the women of Wyoming: "Drop us if you must," it read. "We can trust the men of Wyoming to enfranchise us again after our territory becomes a state."

The second was from the men of the Wyoming legislature. It read: "We may stay out of the Union 100 years, but we will come in with our women!" The suffrage law remained and Wyoming was admitted to the Union—voting women and all!

If you visit Statuary Hall in the United States Capitol, you'll see fifty statues, one from each state, standing in a circle. Forty-nine of them are men. The fiftieth is Esther Morris proudly representing Wyoming, the Equality State.

HELPFUL SOURCES

Books and magazines:

Anthony, Susan B., et al. *The History of Woman Suffrage*, vol. IV. Indianapolis: Hollenbeck Press, 1902.

Cheney, Lynne. "It All Started in Wyoming" in *American Heritage Magazine*, April 1973.

Dobler, Lavinia. *Esther Morris: First Woman Justice of the Peace*. Riverton, Wyoming: Big Bend Press, 1993.

Harper, Ida Husted, et al. *The History of Woman Suffrage*, vol V. New York: National American Woman Suffrage Association, 1922.

Larson, T. A. *History of Wyoming*. New York: Putnam, 1951.

Massie, Michael A. "The Roots of Woman Suffrage in Wyoming" in *Annals of Wyoming*, Spring 1990.

Sherlock, James L. *South Pass and Its Tales*. Basin, Wyoming: Wolverine Gallery, 1978.

Stanton, Elizabeth Cady, et al. *The History of Woman Suffrage*, vol III: Rochester, New York: Susan B. Anthony Press, 1881.

Collections of old letters, papers, and photographs:

Grace R. Hebard papers. Western Historical Research Center, University of Wyoming, Laramie, Wyoming.

Wyoming State Archives, Cheyenne, Wyoming

Websites:

Art in the U.S. Capitol
http://www.aoc.gov/art/nshpages/morris.htm

Nineteenth Amendment
http://www.nara.gov/exhall/charters/constitution/19th/19thhtml

Women of the West Museum
http://www.wowmuseum.org/gallery/suffrage-wy.html

PLACES TO VISIT

Fremont County Pioneer Museum, Lander, Wyoming.

South Pass City Historic Site, South Pass City, Wyoming.